FOUR I ̄ ̄ ̄ ̄ ̄
JEW

Football, Fans and Faith

JEWISH
MUSEUM
LONDON

SHIRE PUBLICATIONS

Published in Great Britain in 2013 by Shire Publications Ltd,
PO Box 883, Oxford, OX1 9PL, UK
PO Box 3985, New York, NY 10185-3985, USA
E-mail: shire@shirebooks.co.uk   www.shirebooks.co.uk

A CIP catalogue record for this book is available from the
British Library.

ISBN-13: 978 0 74781 441 2

Joanne Rosenthal, David Dee, Anthony Clavane, David
Goldblatt and David Conn have has asserted their rights
under the Copyright, Designs and Patents Act, 1988, to be
identified as the author of their contributions.

Designed by Myriam Bell Design, UK and typeset in
Perpetua and Futura.
Editor Ruth Sheppard.

Printed in the UK through Charlesworth Press.

13 14 15 16 17   10 9 8 7 6 5 4 3 2 1

COVER IMAGE
Claude Cohen of Mile End Old Boys' football team, 1906.
(Jewish Museum London)

TITLE PAGE IMAGE
Barry Silkman in action for Manchester City at Maine Road,
1979. (Colorsport)

CONTENTS PAGE IMAGE
Charlton players in training, c. 1921.

PHOTOGRAPH ACKNOWLEDGEMENTS
Images supplied courtesy of:
The family of Harry Blacker, page 23; City of London,
London Metropolitan Archives, page 18; Getty Images,
page 22; Manchester Jewish Museum, pages 30, 44, 45,
46; National Football Museum, page 47; Barry Pincus,
page 19; Leslie Silver, page 39; Harold Summers, page 34.

ACKNOWLEDGEMENTS
The Jewish Museum would like to thank all those who
have generously supported this exhibition.

Shire Publications is supporting the Woodland Trust, the UK's leading woodland conservation charity, by funding the dedication of trees.

CONTENTS

INTRODUCTION

'I am now convinced that the Jews have taken up soccer in a most whole-hearted way.'

Daily Express, 1934

*F*OUR FOUR JEW: FOOTBALL, FANS AND FAITH explores the many ways that Britain's Jews have – in the above words of sports correspondent Trevor Wignall – 'taken up' the beautiful game.

The exhibition both celebrates the contribution Jews have made to the world of football, on and off the field, and considers what football has given to British Jews. The national game has offered Jews a means of integration and the opportunity to transcend ethnic or religious divisions through belonging to a wider community. Tracing the story from Association Football's roots in the late nineteenth century to the modern game we know today, *Four Four Jew* frames the Jewish story in the context of football and vice versa. Given this historical scope it is fitting that we are staging the exhibition in the year that the Football Association celebrates its 150th anniversary, under the chairmanship of David Bernstein.

In recent years there has been a growing interest in the subject of Jews and football. A 1996 study by the Institute for Jewish Policy Research found that Jews were nearly twice as likely to be football fans as the general population.[1] More recently, the subject has been the focus of both academic and non-academic study, with David Dee[2] of Leicester De Montfort University, and sports writer Anthony Clavane[3] publishing books that look deeper at the connections between Jews and football. Both writers have contributed generously to the exhibition's development and both are featured in this book.

1. 'The Flip Side of British Jewry', *Jewish Chronicle* (1 March 1996).
2. David Dee, *Sport and British Jewry* (Manchester University Press, 2013).
3. Anthony Clavane, *Does Your Rabbi Know You're Here* (Quercus, 2012).

Opposite: Albert Goodman in action for Charlton Athletic, c. 1921.

Four Four Jew evolved in the context of this growing interest. It was clear that there was an appetite for this story to be told. For the Jewish Museum, this exhibition offers an exciting opportunity to extend our mission of celebrating and exploring Jewish culture and heritage into a completely new arena.

Part of the joy of putting this exhibition together has been searching for the material to tell the stories we knew needed to be told. Football is experienced in the moment, whether at the pub, in the stadium, or on the pitch and football stories live in these moments. Exhibitions, on the other hand, are based primarily on what is tangible, so it has been a challenge – an enjoyable one – to find this material.

Most of the items the exhibition brings together have never been seen publicly before and few could be termed conventional 'museum' objects. They come from attics and bedrooms, as much, if not more so, as libraries and archives. We are grateful to all the object donors – former players, managers, chairmen, and of course fans of all persuasions – for their generosity in allowing us to share their stories. A selection of highlights from the exhibition feature in this book, with extended captions.

Equally exciting has been the opportunity to explore the Museum's own collection in a way that has never been done before – through the lens of football. Like all museums, we are only able to put a small fraction of our collection on permanent display; most of it is stored away from public view.

Medals of the Victoria Boys' and Girls' clubs.

Tottenham Hotspur club photo, 1919–20. Albert Goodman is on back row, far left.

Trawling through our photographic archives and object stores has been a revelation, bringing to light various treasures that were crucial to shaping the narrative of *Four Four Jew*.

One of my favourite discoveries was a set of rare photographs documenting the career of Albert (or Abraham) Goodman, one of the earliest Jewish footballers ever to play professionally in Britain. Donated to the museum in the 1980s by a family member, the photographs span the breadth of Goodman's football career, from his schoolboy days captaining London Fields FC, to the pinnacle of his career at Tottenham Hotspur and Charlton Athletic. We are delighted to be displaying them as part of the wider mosaic we have assembled showcasing Jewish players who 'made it' as professionals.

The story of Jews and football is a rich and multi-layered one. *Four Four Jew* explores four key narratives.

We take as our starting point the mass migration of Eastern European Jews in the late nineteenth century, which had a cataclysmic effect on the Anglo-Jewish community. The settled British-Jewish elites assumed a responsibility to integrate or 'anglicise' these Russian and Polish Jews, and the East End youth clubs that were established as a result form a big part of this story. The Museum has rich material on these youth clubs, many of which we feature here, as a way of showing how sport, and more

Above: Page from
Victoria Boys' Club
photograph album,
1934–39.

Right: Football
team poem from
Dempsey Street
School magazine,
December 1928.

now the left half's a problem with that you'll agree.
The chap that plays there why Nieman must be;
And can't you just feel how happy he'll be
When we get our team to the top of the tree.

Of Kovalsky our centre I should say a lot,
Our opponents all know he's a terrific shot;
And yet if he took all the chances he got,
When he kicked the ball the goalie'd feel hot.

Our inside left Ockenoff a fine fellow is he,
A chap that 'I'd go a long way to see;
And then when I have him in front of me
I look at his tricks and chuckle with glee.

Our outside left Schneider is only just new,
But players of his there are very few;
He's fast and he's clever at dodging right through,
So give him his chance he'll turn out real blue.

Now Applebaum our captain about him I won't swank,
He's as difficult to pass as a twenty foot tank;
And often when opponents have drawn a blank,
Well it's his mighty efforts that we have to thank.

-----------oOo-----------

specifically football, featured in this 'anglicising' project.

The second layer is the story of the fans. Football is a tribal sport, offering a sense of belonging that can cut across societal divisions – class, ethnicity, race, religion. As such, it played an important role for first-generation immigrants, offering a route into a new community. We explore these themes through the stories of a selection of fans, each of whom inherited different football allegiances alongside their Jewish identity. In the third section we take this further, exploring football's religious dimension as well as the conflicts between football and Judaism.

The exhibition culminates in a celebration of Jewish football achievements on and off the field. Despite common misconceptions, Jews have played the game at the highest level from the turn of the twentieth century to the present day. We are delighted to be showcasing eleven players who represent this journey.

M. Lazarus *(Orient)*

Mark Lazarus cigarette card, c. 1970. Born in the East End of London to a boxing family, Lazarus had a successful career, which included spells at Rangers, Leyton Orient, Wolverhampton Wanderers and Crystal Palace. He is best known for scoring the winning goal at Wembley for Queens Park Rangers in the 1967 League Cup final.

The Jewish contribution off the field has of course been monumental. We have covered this through the stories of celebrated Jewish writers such as Henry Rose and Brian Glanville; revolutionary figures such as David Dein, who transformed his club as vice-chairman and went on to transform the face of football through his role in the establishment of the Premier League; and many more. As is always the case, much has been left out but we hope the exhibition serves as a fitting tribute to this contribution.

There's no greater example of teamwork than putting together an exhibition and there are several people to whom thanks are due here. Firstly, to the contributors to this publication – Anthony Clavane, David Conn, David Dee and David Goldblatt – whose articles draw on the exhibition's themes, offering new insights full of warmth, wit and wisdom. And secondly to the exhibition's advisors, without whom *Four Four Jew* would not have been possible – David Bernstein, Anthony Clavane, David Dein, David Pleat, Lord Triesman, Kick it Out, the Manchester Jewish Museum and the National Football Museum. We are grateful to all for their generosity, lasting support and invaluable guidance.

Joanne Rosenthal
Curator, *Four Four Jew: Football, Fans and Faith*

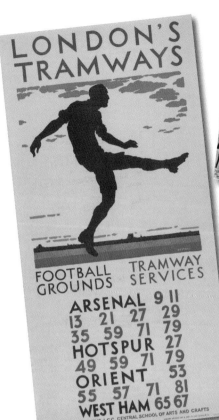

LONDON'S TRAMWAYS

FOOTBALL GROUNDS — TRAMWAY SERVICES

ARSENAL 9 11
13 21 27 29
35 59 71 79
HOTSPUR 27
49 59 71 79
ORIENT 53
55 57 71 81
WEST HAM 65 67

DESIGNED AT THE L.C.C. CENTRAL SCHOOL OF ARTS AND CRAFTS

1958

SEASON 1965-66

Arsenal
FOOTBALL CLUB

FOOTBALL LEAGUE
DIVISION ONE

Saturday,
25th September
v.
Manchester United

KICK-OFF 3 P.M.

OFFICIAL PROGRAMME

6d

NERO

Marv will be at six o'clock tonight and March
of the Day at ten on BBC1

JEWISH ATHLETIC ASSOCIATION TICKET, 1925

This match ticket is from a game between East London Boys and Yarmouth Boys on 17 April 1925. The game was organised by the Jewish Athletic Association (JAA) and took place at the home ground of Clapton Orient Football Club (now Leyton Orient).

The JAA was founded in London in 1899 to promote sporting opportunities for young working-class Jews. It served as the coordinating body for the many sports clubs that were already in existence and organised competitions on Sundays to enable Sabbath-observant Jews to play football. One of the association's objectives was to develop good relations between Jews and non-Jews. To this end several JAA clubs participated in non-Jewish football competitions.

In 1900 the JAA established a football league with six teams: Brady Street Club for Working Boys, the Endearment Jewish Cricket Club, Jews' Free School, the 'Old Boys' of the Norwood Jews Orphanage, South London Lads' Club and West Central Jewish Lads' Club.

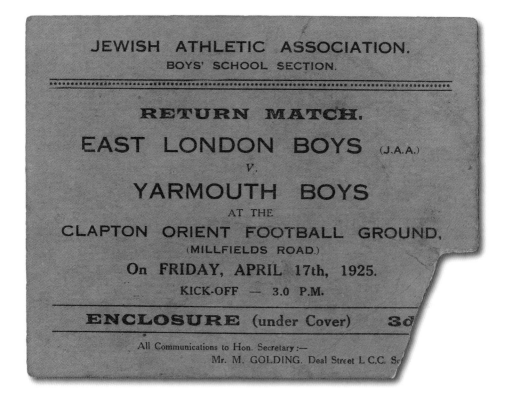

Jews Free School
football team with
the Paul Howard
Football Cup,
1907.

Football team
of the Norwood
Jewish Orphanage,
1930s.

In 1927 the JAA merged with the Central Council of Jewish Boys' and Young Men's Institutions to become the Association of Jewish Youth, which organised Sunday league football in the United Kingdom for nearly a century.

WINGATE SUPPORTERS CLUB

In association with

WINGATE FOOTBALL CLUB

(London League Premier and First Divisions)

Patron:
Lord Nathan
of
Churt
P.C., D.L.

President:
Jack Solomons, Esq.

Vice-President:
Bud Flanagan, Esq.

Do You know . .

that Wingate Football Club is the only Jewish Club in the Country playing Senior League Football.

You are Cordially invited . .

to become a regular Patron at our matches . .

EVERY SATURDAY AFTERNOON

at Maccabi Stadium, Hall Lane, Watford Way, Hendon, N.W.4

113 Bus from Hendon Central Tube Station passes the Ground

Look for match announcements in Hendon & Finchley Times and all the local press, also our posters on the Tube Stations.

Printed by Albert Robins & Co. Ltd., 334 Essex Road, London, N.1— CAN 6771

WINGATE SUPPORTERS CLUB FLYER

This flyer was produced by the Wingate Supporters Club in the 1960s. It belongs to the author Clive Sinclair who was a fan of the club, and who wrote a short story on Wingate in his book *Hearts of Gold*. Sinclair's father was the chairman of the Supporters Club.

Wingate Football Club was an all-Jewish club founded in 1946 by British Jewish ex-servicemen, in response to the growing fascist presence in 1940s London. The founders believed that 'fascism could be fought better on the football field than with fists'. The club was named after Major Orde Wingate, a non-Jewish British Army general, who worked with the Jewish Defence Forces in British Mandate Palestine.

Wingate was proud of its Jewish identity and hoped to combat rising anti-Semitism through positive, sportsmanlike engagement with non-Jewish teams in the Football League. The team played in blue and white with Stars of David on their kits and had many players on their books that went on to have successful careers as professionals in the higher leagues.

In 1991 Wingate merged with Finchley Football Club to become Wingate and Finchley FC.

Loaned by Clive Sinclair

MACCABI TICKET AND MEDAL, 1964

This ticket and medal are from a benefit match between Maccabi Association London and an all-star team of former Tottenham Hotspur players.

Maccabi organised the match in honour of John White, a Tottenham player who was killed in a freak accident in the prime of his career. The game drew record crowds and took place at Maccabi Stadium, which was also Wingate's home ground.

Spurs legend Danny Blanchflower captained the ex-Spurs team, months after his retirement as a player. Also playing were former Jewish players Micky Dulin and Leon Joseph as well as eight others from the 1950/51 First Division Championship-winning side. Medals were presented by singer Frankie Vaughan, who himself had enjoyed a career in football, signing for Wingate in the 1950s.

Maccabi Association London (North West London Maccabi) were a successful Jewish Sunday league team who played in the Hendon & District Sunday Football League. The team's coaches included well-known names, such as Arsenal centre forwards Cliff Holton and Vic Groves, and Terry Venables, just sixteen years of age at the time and in his first coaching job.

Ticket loaned by Clive Sinclair; medal loaned by Ken Goldman

SECOND WORLD WAR BRITISH AIR RAID PRECAUTIONS GAS RATTLE, 1939

This wooden rattle is one of many used on the streets of London to warn people of a possible gas attack during the Second World War.

Rabbi Tony Bayfield inherited the rattle from his grandfather as a young boy. He chalked it in the colours of West Ham United – claret and blue – and used it as a football rattle in the terraces of Upton Park. The rattle has now taken on another function in the Bayfield family, and is used as a *gregger* during the festival of Purim.

There is a long tradition of wooden rattles being used at football games, stretching back to the late nineteenth century. Originally used to announce the end of factory shifts, the rattles were adapted for use by football fans and often customised according to the colours of one's team.

Loaned by Rabbi Tony Bayfield

LONDON TRAMWAYS POSTER – ROUTES TO GAMES, 1925

This poster was designed at the Central School of Arts and Crafts by E. B. Stall. It shows the tram routes to Arsenal, Leyton Orient, Tottenham Hotspur and West Ham. All four of these London clubs developed significant Jewish fan bases in the interwar years, which remain to this day.

Public transport played a big role in the development of Jewish fan bases at football clubs. Large Jewish communities in the East End of London and those who had begun to move out northwards and eastwards were local to the clubs featured in this poster. For many, participating in the local ritual of watching live football became as much a part of the Sabbath as attending synagogue services.

Writing in a letter to *The Jewish Chronicle*, a Tottenham Hotspur fan explained how his attachment to the club grew in the 1920s: 'It was possible to be in synagogue until the end of musaf, to nip home for a quick plate of lokshen soup, and then to board a tram from Aldgate to White Hart Lane. No other ground could offer such ease of access.'

Harry Pincus with son Barry outside the family home in Highbury. Growing up in the East End of London, Harry was able to travel easily to Arsenal matches to watch his team. As an adult living in Highbury, he was just a short walk from the stadium.

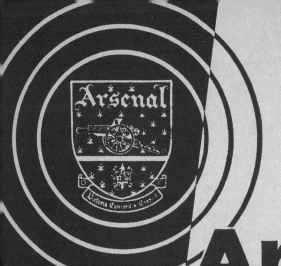

SEASON 1965-66

Arsenal
FOOTBALL CLUB

F.A. CUP WINNERS
1930, 1936, 1950

LEAGUE CHAMPIONS
1931, 1933, 1934, 1935,
1938, 1948, 1953

FOOTBALL LEAGUE
DIVISION ONE

Saturday,

25th September

v.

Manchester United

KICK-OFF 3 P.M.

6d

OFFICIAL PROGRAMME

ARSENAL PROGRAMME, 1965

In this match programme, Arsenal note that kick-off for their next fixture has been moved to a later time 'to assist our many Jewish supporters who will be observing Rosh Hashana.'

This is the first time that Arsenal wished their Jewish fans a Happy New Year in official club literature. It is interesting to note that, despite often being considered a 'Jewish club', it wasn't until 1973 that Tottenham Hotspur did the same.

Since the 1930s Arsenal have had a very strong Jewish following and nurtured their relationship with this section of their fan base, rearranging matches to avoid festivals and apologising when clashes occurred.

Loaned by Harry Klahr

Vol. XLVII. No. 4   Saturday, 25th September, 1965

Voice of Arsenal

"WHAT has happened to Manchester United?" was the question being asked after the first two or three matches this season. A very good answer came last Saturday when Matt Busby's team scored an overwhelming win against Chelsea to the tune of 4-1. Man of the Match was Denis Law with a hat-trick. There is little doubt that United are back to peak form and as we nearly always get a fine match when we play them, this afternoon's meeting could produce a classic. After our double over Nottingham Forest, which was an excellent performance, we must not be too disappointed over our defeat at Everton last Saturday. We would be the first to admit that Everton were the better side on the day, but we lost the afternoon within the space of three minutes when two mistakes in quick succession cost us a goal each time. When Everton got a third in the second-half the task was nearly hopeless but we did manage to pull one goal back through Joe Baker, although both Joe and George Eastham were feeling the

effects of knocks. Incidentally, we were compelled to make a team change on Saturday morning because David Court was not feeling well; we could have taken a chance and played him but it is rarely

ARSENAL v. NORTHAMPTON
Tuesday, 28th September

IN order to assist our many Jewish supporters who will be observing Rosh Hashana (New Year) on 27th and 28th September the kick-off for the above game will be 7.45 p.m. At the same time we would like to take the opportunity of wishing them all a very happy New Year.

wise to do this sort of thing so Peter Simpson took his place. David changed as a substitute as we felt he was capable of playing part of a match if it became necessary whereas ninety minutes would probably have been too much for him.

2

PHOTOGRAPH OF ENGLAND vs GERMANY INTERNATIONAL FRIENDLY, 1935

On 4 December 1935, England played Germany in the first international friendly between the teams since Hitler came to power. White Hart Lane, home ground of Tottenham Hotspur, was chosen as the venue for the game.

Given the broad Jewish fan base at the club, many Jews were outraged and, together with Trade Unionists and anti-fascist campaigners, petitioned the English Football Association to cancel the match. Despite the level of public debate on the issue, the match went ahead peacefully and England won 3-0.

In this photograph of the match in action, a swastika flag can be seen on the right, flying over the stadium.

Tottenham Hotspur's Jewish fan base first developed in the early twentieth century and, as is the case with Arsenal, remains very strong to this day. Newspaper reports covering the 1935 match noted that at that point, roughly one-third of the club's home support was Jewish.

Mariv will be at six o'clock tonight and Match of the Day at ten on BBC1

HARRY BLACKER CARTOON

Harry Blacker was a cartoonist and illustrator who worked under the name Nero.

Born in Whitechapel in 1910 to Eastern European immigrant parents, he designed posters for London Transport, the Post Office, Shell and BP, and was published in many publications including *Punch*, *Bystander* and *The Jewish Chronicle*.

Football is a recurring subject in his Jewish-themed cartoons, and Blacker often drew humour through gently satirising the Jewish love of the beautiful game. In another Nero cartoon, a young boy threatens his mother with the words, 'If you won't let me watch Chelsea next Saturday, I'm going to become a Rabbi instead of a brain surgeon.'

LOUIS BOOKMAN MEDAL, 1913

This medal was awarded to Louis Bookman following an exhibition match between Bradford City and Manchester United. The match took place at Belfast Celtic as part of Bookman's transfer deal from Celtic to Bradford.

Louis Bookman was the first Jewish footballer to play professionally, and the first to gain international honours. A Lithuanian-born immigrant to Ireland, he represented his adopted country four times and had a successful career at club level, playing for Bradford City, West Bromwich Albion, and Luton Town.

Born Louis Buchalter, he opted to be known as Bookman in his footballing life as it was easier for his teammates to pronounce. A multi-talented sportsman who excelled at both football and cricket, as a young boy Bookman played for Adelaide, a Jewish youth team named after the Adelaide Road synagogue in Dublin.

Loaned by Joyce Levy

D. H. MORRIS CIGARETTE CARD, 1927

David Hyman (Harry) Morris was a professional footballer, born in the East End of London in 1897. He attended the Jews Free School and was a member of the Brady Street Boys' Club.

Morris was a prolific goalscorer and played for several clubs including Fulham, Millwall, Swansea and Swindon Town. For seven consecutive seasons (1926–33), Morris was Swindon's leading goalscorer. He still holds the Swindon records for most goals in a league match, season and career.

Despite playing on Saturdays, Morris was known as an observant Jew and refused to play on high holidays.

This cigarette card was issued during Morris's second season at Swindon, and is part of a set featuring fifty notable players of the day.

DAVID PLEAT MACCABIAH MEDAL, 1961

In 1961 David Pleat represented Britain at the Maccabiah Games in Israel. This gold medal was awarded to Pleat following Britain's victory in the final of the football tournament. At the time he was playing for Nottingham Forest's youth team.

David Pleat is a hugely well-established figure in British football, whose career spans over fifty years. He has enjoyed success at all levels of the game as player, manager, scout, commentator and sports columnist. In the 1980s, as manager, he transformed Luton Town into a major club in English football. In 2012 Pleat was inducted into the League Managers Association Hall of Fame.

Born in Nottingham, Pleat's family originated from Poland and Latvia, immigrating to London and changing their name from Plotz. His father, whose passions included drama, boxing and football, was a member of the Oxford and St George's Jewish Lads' Club in Whitechapel.

Loaned by David Pleat

CLUB PHOTOGRAPH OF ASTON VILLA, 1896

This Aston Villa team won the League and Cup double in the 1896/7 season. The club's chairman at that time was Joshua Margoschis, a local tobacconist. He features in the photo on the back row, far right.

Margoschis is thought to be the first Jewish chairman of a British football club, and as such serves as an early example of Jewish involvement in football at boardroom level.

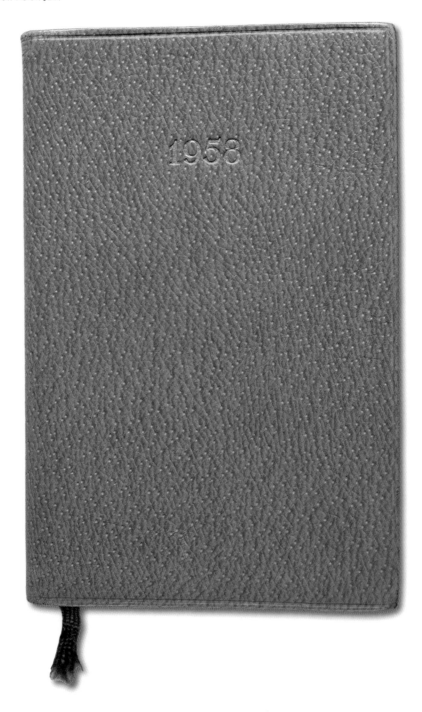

DIARY OF DAVID DEIN, 1958

David Dein is the former vice-chairman of Arsenal Football Club and the Football Association. He is widely recognised as one of the most influential figures in modern football, revolutionising his own club, and – as an architect of the Premier League – British football itself.

As a teenager, Dein kept a detailed diary that recorded everything from his own playing days in north-west London to family gatherings, cinema outings, and match reports of his beloved Arsenal and many other games. The diary captures Dein's passion for football, which spanned all competitions and leagues – Maccabi as well as the then First Division.

The page featured here shows Dein's reaction to the Munich Air Disaster of February 1958. The accounts relating to Munich are written in red ink, highlighting the shock he felt in response to the unfolding tragedy.

Loaned by David Dein

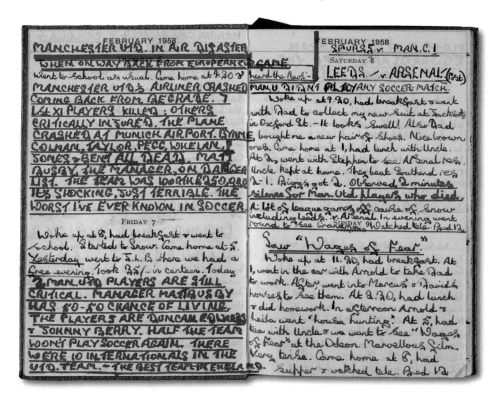

'IRONING OUT THE GHETTO BEND': FOOTBALL, INTEGRATION AND JEWISH 'ANGLICISATION'

DAVID DEE

In 1903, an article entitled 'True Sportsmanship' appeared in *The Bradian*, the magazine of the Brady Street Club for Working Boys, founded in 1896 in Whitechapel for use by local Jews. The author exclaimed that 'the aim of everyone who plays a game of any kind, be it cricket or football, is to be known as a good player and a good sportsman'. Club members were told to 'learn to "play the game" in a good wholesome spirit… and you will derive great pleasure and physical benefits from doing so'.

Such instructions for youth club members involved in sport would have been commonplace at this time, but for the Jews attending Brady Street they took on special significance. Founded in the heart of the Jewish immigrant East End of London, Brady was the first of several clubs opened to cater for young Jews hailing from the Russian and Eastern European migrant population that settled in London from the 1880s until 1914. Clubs like Brady Street, the West Central Jewish Working Lads' Club (founded 1898), Stepney Jewish Lads' Club (1900), Victoria Jewish Lads' Club (1901), Hutchison House (1905), Notting Hill Jewish Lads' Club (1908) and the Oxford and St George's Club (1914) were all patronised by the English-Jewish 'Cousinhood' (such as the Rothschilds and Waley-Cohens) with philanthropy for the purpose of 'Anglicisation' as their common aim.

Opposite: Member of Grove House Lads Club Football Team, 1932.

Right: Victoria Boys' Club football trophy. The names of the awardees from 1957 to 1985 are inscribed on the base.

A.KRAVITZ 1957-58
A."KRAVITZ 1958-59
D. DEEN 1959-60
H. STANTON 1960-61
J. ROSE. 1961-62
G.LYONS. 1962-63
N.BITTON 1963-64
N.BITTON 1964-65
R.ROOD 1965-66
S.SACK 1966-67
L.BLAIBERG 1967-68
D.VERNON 1968-69
B.LEITER 1970-71

Jewish Athletic
Association medal,
1914. Loaned by
Ken Goldman.

Maccabi football
medal, 1962.
Loaned by Ken
Goldman.

At a time of growing 'anti-Alienism', the Jewish youth movement — which also encompassed several girls clubs and the Jewish Lads' Brigade (founded in 1895) — prioritised sport as a means of helping young Jews think, act and look more like their Gentile peers. As the national game, football was given precedence and was seen to have distinct 'Anglicising' benefits. In the first instance, getting young Jews to play soccer was seen as one way of 'ironing out the Ghetto bend' amongst those with seemingly stunted and weak physiques — a legacy of life in the Russian Pale. Training sessions, inter-club leagues and competitions organised by the Jewish Athletic Association from 1899 onwards helped to improve fitness and strength among club members.

Alongside combating accusations of 'alien degeneracy' and weakness, football was employed as a medium for inculcating 'British' characteristics and mores into the youngsters. Upper-class Jewish patrons and middle-class, often public-schooled, club managers and volunteers saw soccer as a way of 'grafting' Britishness onto Jews of migrant heritage. Regular lectures, talks and articles (like the one above) were produced instructing young Jewish footballers on the values of sportsmanship, fair play and teamwork; notions embedded in an idealised form of Britishness. In a similar vein, 'unsporting' behaviour was admonished and seen to be indicative of the retention of 'foreign' personality traits. In 1904, for instance, the Stepney Jewish Club Chronicle lamented reports of 'rough play' and poor sportsmanship by club footballers and spectators at a recent match. Club managers bemoaned the fact that this 'did not say much for the boys as sportsmen' and indicated behaviour not befitting young Britons.

Despite this, the youth movement had a great deal of success in using sports like football for 'Anglicisation'. Government reports into the nation's fitness published in 1904 praised Jewish organisations for their work at improving migrant health through sport. One witness reported that his belief that the 'Jewish child... is as a rule a stronger and healthier child than the Gentile'. Social investigations into the pre-First World War East

End also praised Jewish clubs for their concentration on the 'physical improvement of their members' through sport and noted that football aided the 'transformation' of young 'alien' physiques.

Similarly, club members also praised soccer for its 'character-building' qualities and saw it as a 'training ground for citizenship'. One alumnus of the West Central club later recalled: 'It sounds like a little thing, but if you lost a football match, you learned to say "Well

MARCH, 1913.

THE HUTCH

A MAGAZINE DEVOTED TO THE INTERESTS OF THE MEMBERS OF THE HUTCHISON HOUSE CLUB FOR WORKING LADS

PLAY THE GAME

CONTENTS

New Series.

Vol. II., No. I.

Front cover of *The Hutch*, magazine of Hutchison House Club for Working Lads, March 1913.

Major Harvey Sadow (with pipe), one of the founders of Wingate Football Club, with the London Maccabi football team, 1938.

played" to your opponents and go on your way. No bitterness, no fighting and no arguments and that is hard for a pugnacious boy to do. However, we were told that was the way it had to be. If you lose, you lose. Someone is going to beat you. Those lessons were priceless.'

The notion of sport being useful in building character and fostering integration at a time of anti-Jewish sentiment emerges elsewhere during the twentieth century. For instance, within the British Maccabi movement football became closely linked to the physical and moral development of members. Founded in 1934, the British Maccabi Association believed deeply in the promotion of 'Muscular Judaism' through sport as a means of supporting the Zionist cause. Within the BMA, football became an extremely popular activity, with a national league being founded in 1936 for member clubs.

Like the youth movement before 1914, Maccabi in the 1930s stressed the physical and psychological benefits of sport for young Jews. In the same decade that Mosley's British Union of Fascists promoted notions of Jewish 'physical, mental and moral difference', British Maccabi leaders were promoting football as a means of imbuing 'the highest qualities of discipline, morality and sportsmanship' into members. In 1936, the year of the Battle of Cable Street, the organisation published the 'Maccabi Code', calling on members to 'follow the ideal of Judas Maccabaeus by proving yourself physically and morally courageous and fearless, both on and off the field'. Evidently, at a difficult time in British Jewry's modern history, football was viewed as a way of both developing and demonstrating 'Britishness'.

Football also emerged as a means of indicating Jewish integration and 'Anglicisation' in the era immediately following the Second World War. Growing tensions between Britain and the Yishuv, post-war austerity and the re-emergence of British fascist groups led to a growth of anti-Semitism, culminating in anti-Jewish rioting and violence across the country in 1947. Against this backdrop several Jewish ex-servicemen formed Wingate FC in North London in 1946, feeling that they 'could fight anti-Semitism better in sport than by talking about it'. By entering a Jewish team into the amateur Saturday leagues, Wingate's founders believed that football could help 'foster between Jew and Gentile a greater spirit of comradeship', undermine Jewish stereotypes and demonstrate the 'sportsmanship' – and, by extension the 'Britishness' – of the community. Wingate enjoyed modest sporting success, yet developed an award-winning reputation for fair play and friendliness.

Evidently, throughout a large part of modern British-Jewish history, football has been much more than a simple leisure activity. It has been cherished as a means of promoting integration and 'Anglicisation' amongst the community. On the one hand, the sport played a key role in changing the way many Jews regarded and expressed themselves. Significantly, however, soccer also impacted on the way the community was viewed by non-Jewish society.

David Dee is a lecturer in Modern History at De Montfort University, Leicester. He has written and spoken widely on the sporting history of British Jews and is the author of *Sport and British Jewry: Integration, Ethnicity and Anti-Semitism, 1890–1970*, published by Manchester University Press in January 2013.

L. GOLDBERG (LEEDS UNITED)

REBBE IN THE MORNING, REVIE IN THE AFTERNOON

ANTHONY CLAVANE

OVER THE PAST COUPLE OF YEARS, I have been turning into my mother. Let me explain. As a kid, whenever a person of distinction was mentioned – on the box or in the papers – my mum would point out their Jewishness. It was like that *Goodness Gracious Me* sketch in which a character claims that everything comes from India. Whether it was Sigmund Freud or Clement Freud, Sir Ludwig Guttmann, who established the Paralympic Games, or Joseph Malin, who invented fish and chips – the person of distinction would be outed with the cry: 'Jewish!'

Much closer to home, there was Michael Marks, who set up a stall in Leeds 129 years ago. According to legend, my great-grandfather, Solomon Saipe, had a trestle table next to his at the city market. It was oh-so-agonisingly close to being Marks and Saipe rather than Marks and Spencer.

More importantly, to my football-obsessed mind, Leeds United had been oh-so-agonisingly close to boasting the first ever Jewish England player. Leslie Goldberg anyone? Not a name you will recognise, but in the 1930s he was highly regarded enough to be featured in a series of cigarette cards alongside Stanley Matthews, Raich Carter and Cliff Bastin.

In 1937, Leslie replaced the England full back Bert Sproston at Elland Road. He was strongly tipped to replace Sproston at international level; he had already represented the Three Lions at schoolboy level, making his debut at Wembley against Wales in 1932. A reporter at that match described him as possessing a 'very brainy game, depending upon clever anticipation, sure tackling and strong volleying'. As a columnist in a Jewish newspaper wrote: 'It is the sincerest hope of Leeds fans, and I have no doubt Jewish football followers throughout

Opposite and below: Leslie Goldberg Churchman's cigarette card.

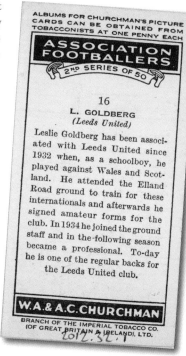

ALBUMS FOR CHURCHMAN'S PICTURE
CARDS CAN BE OBTAINED FROM
TOBACCONISTS AT ONE PENNY EACH

ASSOCIATION
FOOTBALLERS

2ND SERIES OF 50

16

L. GOLDBERG
(*Leeds United*)

Leslie Goldberg has been associated with Leeds United since 1932 when, as a schoolboy, he played against Wales and Scotland. He attended the Elland Road ground to train for these internationals and afterwards he signed amateur forms for the club. In 1934 he joined the ground staff and in the following season became a professional. To-day he is one of the regular backs for the Leeds United club.

W.A. & A.C. CHURCHMAN

BRANCH OF THE IMPERIAL TOBACCO CO.
(OF GREAT BRITAIN & IRELAND), LTD.

the country share this wish, that Leslie Goldberg will one day play for Leeds United and England, and if this does happen may he serve as magnificently as a man as he did as a schoolboy international.' Unfortunately, this didn't happen because war broke out. At the end of the conflict he was transferred to Reading, changed his name to Gaunt and broke his leg.

In researching my book, *Does Your Rabbi Know You're Here?*, I discovered a lot more of these previously untold stories. Of course, it doesn't matter what religion or ethnicity you are. But, as with my mum, the 'outing' process gave me great nachas. One of my favourite stories, as recalled by Goldberg's teammate Izzy Pear, involved Les single-handedly leading his mainly Jewish team to the final of the Leeds Schools Cup. He was injured, missed the match and the team were hammered. Many in the crowd, who had only come to see the Great Goldberg, demanded their money back.

This story illustrated the major theme of my book; through football – a life-long passion for many generations of Jewish fans – we have successfully, if quietly, integrated into English society. The sport was one of the ways my grandparents shed the 'ghetto mentality' of Old World shtetls and transcended the parochialism of an often-insular community. In fact, the story of Leeds United has, in many ways, been the story of Leeds' Jews.

When the latter arrived in the late nineteenth century, there was no football team, but the second-generation immigrants in the Leylands ghetto enthusiastically supported the local rugby league side. United were formed in 1919 in the offices of a Jewish solicitor, Alf Masser. As the community migrated from the grim streets of Chapeltown to the lower-middle-class suburb of Moortown, United themselves became upwardly mobile, transformed from a struggling Second Division outfit to the most feared team in Europe. This was all down, of course, to manager Don Revie. But the club would have sunk into oblivion had three Jewish businessmen – Manny Cussins, Sydney Simon and Albert Morris – not responded to a desperate SOS call from the board by making interest-free loans of £10,000.

Does Your Rabbi Know You're Here? covers the whole of English football, but I particularly enjoyed writing the section about my own team. As Ronnie Teeman – a Jewish lawyer who represented players like John Giles, Peter Lorimer and Joe Jordan – put it: 'What could a Jew talk to his non-Jewish workmate about? Religion? No. That was taboo. But he did have something in common and that was sport. It allowed him to communicate and converse.'

I never saw Les Goldberg play, but my dad did – and the hairs on the back of my neck stood on end when I came across a 1938 British Pathé newsreel clip featuring his exploits. In the clip, a plummy-voiced announcer says: 'And we introduce, on the left, Leslie Goldberg, right-back. A footballer, first of all, must be fit, and PT and shadow boxing both help to that end.'

Leeds United's biggest fan in the 1960s and 1970s was Herbert Warner, a jeweller, market-stall holder and friend of the family. Herbie would often be called upon by Revie to entertain the players. He would walk into the changing room and crack a few Jewish jokes and, in hotels the night before a big match, he relaxed Bremner, Charlton and the other players by organising bingo and carpet bowls sessions. In 1972 he was even allowed to display the centenary FA Cup at his market stall after Leeds had beaten Arsenal to win the trophy. My great-grandfather and Michael Marks would have been very proud.

Anthony Clavane is a sports writer and author. He has written two books about Jewish involvement in football. The first, *Promised Land: A Northern Love Story*, was Sports Book of the Year 2011 at the British Sports Book Awards. The second, *Does Your Rabbi Know You're Here?*, was shortlisted for Football Book of the Year for 2013.

Former chairman of Leeds United, Leslie Silver (far left), celebrates winning the First Division in May 1992. Also pictured are manager Howard Wilkinson, managing director Bill Fotherby, and Gordon Strachan. Silver took over as Chairman in 1983 after Manny Cussins retired.

FINDING STANLEY OTTOLENGHI

DAVID GOLDBLATT

THE CONNECTION BETWEEN being Jewish and following football seemed to me to be completely normal. My grandfather read the Tottenham match reports in the *News of the World* with a reverence bordering on the Talmudic. My father, then in the coats and dresses game, used to take me to Morris Keston's Commercial Road showroom where calendars from Israeli charities and Tottenham Hotspur competed for space. Football meant Spurs and Spurs was ours.

My form of study was closer to the Kabalistic. Closing my eyes and putting myself in the centre of my childhood bedroom I can see the rectangular board in front of me. It is about the size of an old broadsheet newspaper and was, perhaps, a table-top or a strange tray of some kind, with rounded corners and a thin lip. The wooden side is facing me; the grey white Formica side is facing the wall. I think of it as a tablet of stone on which I have inscribed, if not the Law itself, then important commentaries upon it – in biro, felt tip and pencil, the former often gouged into the surface – as a range of dates, scores, and information that demonstrate the superiority of Tottenham Hotspur to Arsenal: a mystical but potent collection of top scorers, league tables and fabulous facts.

It's sometime in 1971 or 1972. I'm six or seven and Stanley Ottolenghi is coming to our house. Stanley is my father's old friend. They met in the mid-1950s as apprentices to Teasy-Weasy Raymond, the faux French celebrity hairdresser from Tooting. Two north London Jewish boys doing shampoo and sets in a louche Mayfair salon. The old man is Tottenham, Stanley is Arsenal. Despite this, perhaps because of it, they go to Spurs and Arsenal games together, home and away. They go to both legs of the 1972 UEFA Cup final, between Spurs and Wolves, and tell us how they persuaded a Brummie waitress that the cream they were putting in their coffee was actually going into Bovril.

My tablet is placed on a table in the hall, but it is just one of many diagrams and lists I have created, including one constructed of graph paper stuck

Opposite:
Tottenham Hotspur
kippa (or skullcap).

Programme for Tottenham Hotspur vs Crystal Palace, 28 August 1943. This was the first match attended by Morris Keston, legendary Spurs fan. During the war, Arsenal shared Tottenham Hotspur's home ground, White Hart Lane, as can be seen in the programme notes. Loaned by Morris Keston.

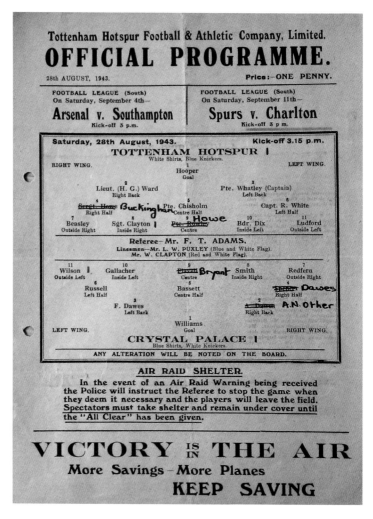

together with sellotape, showing the relative position of the clubs over the season. Stanley walks in, doesn't miss a beat, looks us in the eye and walks out. The old man has to sweet-talk him back into the house and over tea and cigarettes they are lost in conversation and argument and the fate of Sir Alf.

My father never took me to White Hart Lane. By the time I was old enough he was done with going, all the hassle and the fighting. The coats and dresses business went under and the trips to Morris Keston stopped. Stanley and the old man seemed to drift apart. There was still plenty of Judaism around, and plenty of football, but somehow the connection had been lost. Then I found my own Stanley Ottolenghi.

In fact I was spoilt for choice. I know plenty of Spurs fans, Frank the supply teacher, Ollie the mad shrink, Jamaican Roger, but none of them are Jewish. At Arsenal it's another matter. There's Guy from Tel Aviv who sits with the frummers who don't go on Saturdays and whose season tickets I have been known to make use of. Mark, who sometimes has to go to the cinema rather than use his season ticket because the *tsuris* has got all too much. And then there's Daniel.

We met at university, two north London Jewish boys doing politics at a venerable college. He took me to my first game in twenty years – the Arsenal away end at Charlton in 1990. Despite this, or perhaps because of it, we've gone to a lot of games since – at Highbury, the Emirates and White Hart Lane. In a world of globalised football we've made it further than Molineux, meeting up at the European Championships and at two World Cups.

Arsenal *kippa*.

I once sat in the back of a car on our way to a European Championship quarter-final. Dan was driving, actively considering the outcome of the game, and on two different phones negotiating the ground rules of an Israeli–Palestinian peace initiative. On another occasion we met at a Champions League final, Dan with an Israeli ex-minister in tow. After a swift review of the situation in Syria, Lebanon and Gaza he's off looking for the touts.

Dan is infectious, curious and insatiable. He has to be there and more often than not he is. He always has a position, two even, on the game and its meaning, and expects you to have one too. In fact he wants to know what it is. Every conversation somehow comes round to politics, the fate of Arsenal FC or the relatively worse fate of Tottenham Hotspur. Sometimes all three at once. What's not to like?

David Goldblatt was born in London in 1965 and got as far as his pre-clinicals in medicine. He is now a writer, broadcaster and academic. In 2006 he published *The Ball is Round: A Global History of Football*, and teaches at the University of Bristol and Pitzer College Los Angeles.

THE PEOPLE'S GAME?

DAVID CONN

LIKE MANY PEOPLE from all places, backgrounds and generations, I grew up loving football in a way that went beyond mere enjoyment, and dug into the realms of fist-clenched belief. Growing up in north Manchester in the 1970s, the game forged as powerful a role in shaping my world-view as Jewishness itself, the weighty rules and meaty cultural identity into which we were born.

Jewish Manchester City supporters before a match against Grimsby Town, 1936.

Football was what we played, watched hungrily on television or, awestruck, live in a floodlit stadium midweek; the game and its legends were in the air we breathed. We somehow inhaled the knowledge of Matt

Busby and his Manchester United glories, the 1958 Munich air crash that killed eight of his 'babes,' then his epic quest to win the European Cup just ten years later. Not a lot was ever said about Manchester City, the rival sky-blue club which claimed my belonging, winning the Football League championship that same year, 1968. When I was a boy, though, City were not in United's shadow.

Religion was all around us, its rules, formal celebrations and many prohibitions, and looking back, I feel I was blessed with a natural inclination to see the best in it. I always rejected its tribalism of 'us and them', the dogma in the rules, and tended to absorb the good and benevolent messages. I took to heart the story told to us of the famous rabbi asked to sum up the whole of Jewish teaching in the time he could stand on one leg. He delivered that precious nutshell: treat your neighbour as you would like to be treated yourself. As a child, I read that literally: try to be nice to the neighbours.

Later, as I shed layers of religious observance and attended Maine Road on more grey Saturdays, it abided with me: try to be good. As an adult I came to understand that the rabbi's summary was one that would be repeated by decent priests of all religions – that treating others properly is a common value of good human relations.

Henry Rose, celebrated sports journalist for the *Daily Express*. The caption on the back of the photograph reads 'This is one of my favourite pictures, taken outside my hotel in Berlin, when on tour with the England Soccer Touring Team'. Rose was one of two Jews who died in the Munich Air Disaster of 1958, the other being local businessman Willie Satinoff – a Manchester United fan and close friend of Matt Busby.

Manchester City and England goalkeeper Frank Swift presents a cup to Murray Sherman of the Manchester Jewish Soccer League. Swift died in the Munich Air Disaster of 1958.

Negotiating English football's battered landscape in the 1980s – the mudbaths and threats of violence when we played in amateur leagues; the great clubs' run-down grounds, fences around the pitch, the flanks of police horses and outbreaks of fighting – I tended to do the same with the game: see the best of it. Football, for all its incomparable attraction, can be a force for good or bad. It has been, and still is in some places, a rallying opportunity for division along tribal, racial or simply brutish lines; for meanness of spirit, for sour taunting, for bullying, for a mass failure to treat neighbours as we would like to be treated ourselves. I always sided with the opponents of that tendency: believing Pelé when he praised football as the beautiful game, feeling in it something elementally precious, seeing the crowds as people coming together, not divided.

When the money from BSkyB poured into the top division, repackaged as the Premier League in 1992, I thought this 'whole new ball game,' as Sky promised on their billboards, would be all for the good. We would have safe stadiums after the horrors of Hillsborough, football would be accepted as a life-enhancing sport not a filthy habit, the game would be rehabilitated.

That happened, of course. But when, as a journalist, I discovered how the new millions were being carved up, by the 'owners' of clubs looking to make money for themselves, I felt instinctively this was wrong. So I was sent on an investigative journey, learning of the game's public-school roots, the rules – embodying values of sportsmanship and fair play – defined in 1863 by upper-class gentlemen who called themselves the Football Association.

Clubs in working-class areas of late Victorian towns and cities, like my Manchester City, were formed by churches, who saw in football both physical and character-building benefits, to counter the poverty which ransacked the industrial neighbourhoods.

The FA reluctantly allowed players to be paid in 1885 – against the governing body's innate, albeit privileged, ideal that their game should be played only for love. When twelve clubs paying professional players formed the Football League – the world's first ever – in 1888, the FA insisted, with a body of regulations, that the clubs should remain essentially not-for-profit. If they formed limited companies, the directors could not pay themselves salaries, nor the 'owners,' the shareholders, sizeable dividends. This institutionalised the FA's view that football clubs should remain what they had roared into becoming: homes of sporting passion and raucous loyalty, not mere entertainment companies for entrepreneurs to exploit.

Thus I discovered that my gut instinct, ingested in the course of playing and watching the game, was in fact founded on longstanding values the FA had insisted upon from football's beginnings. Club owners' modern machinations and the stock-market floats by which they were seeking to make fortunes for themselves were contrary to football's best tradition and our justified emotional sense that the clubs belonged to us all.

Famous English footballers of 1881 from *Boy's Own* magazine. Four years later, the English Football Association lifted the ban on professionalism in football.

FAMOUS ENGLISH FOOTBALL PLAYERS. 1881.

Many owners of top clubs cashed in hugely in the early years of the twenty-first century, selling these great clubs to buyers from overseas, who had no connections to them, and mixed motives, mostly financial, for buying them up.

A body of opposition has grown to this exploitation of football as an entertainment 'product' by mega-rich owners looking to make yet more money out of the clubs. Campaigners argue for a game which reflects its great, simple truths: that the clubs are really members' organisations which should be owned by their supporters, that tickets should be affordable as they used to be, and money distributed more equally, so that all clubs and sections of society can share in football's wonders.

In sympathising, fist-clenched at times, with this, the people's vision, and rejecting that of the oligarchs, I tend to feel I am siding with the best of football's values. That football as the people's game can embody decent human values, and therefore the best of Jewish values, which I was brought up to believe are important.

David Conn writes about football for *The Guardian*. His book, *Richer than God: Manchester City, Modern Football and Growing Up* (2012), is now available in paperback.